Vincent J. Knapp

State University of New York College
Potsdam

Europe
in the Era of
Social
Transformation

1700-Present

PRENTICE-HALL, INC., ENGLEWOOD CLIFFS, NEW JERSEY

Library of Congress Cataloging in Publication Data

KNAPP, VINCENT J (date)
    Europe in the era of social transformation 1700-
present.

    Bibliography: p.
    Includes index.
    1. Europe—Social conditions. 2. Europe—Economic
conditions. 3. Social classes—Europe—History.
I. Title.
HN373.K48   309.1'4   75-14244
ISBN 0-13-291971-0
ISBN 0-13-291948-6 pbk.

PRENTICE-HALL INTERNATIONAL, INC., LONDON
PRENTICE-HALL OF AUSTRALIA, PTY. LTD., SYDNEY
PRENTICE-HALL OF CANADA, LTD., TORONTO
PRENTICE-HALL OF INDIA PRIVATE LIMITED, NEW DELHI
PRENTICE-HALL OF JAPAN, INC., TOKYO
PRENTICE-HALL OF SOUTHEAST ASIA (PTE.) LTD., SINGAPORE